A Labyrinth Of Emotions

A book about a Deeply Emotional Connection

Monaliza

BookLeaf Publishing

India | USA | UK

Made with ♥ on the BookLeaf Publishing Platform

www.bookleafpub.in

www.bookleafpub.com

Dedication

To my daughter, Tara—May you always walk through life with wonder in your eyes and strength in your heart. And Rohit—For believing in me when I couldn't believe in myself, and for turning impossibilities into steps forward.

To Betty —Your unwavering reassurance has been my anchor and my light. Thank you for always being there.

With all my love,

Preface

This collection of poems is a mirror—sometimes cracked, sometimes clear—held up to the inner landscapes I've wandered through. Each piece is a fragment of my truth, written not to be perfect, but to be honest. These poems came to life in quiet moments and chaotic ones, during heartbreaks and awakenings, in solitude and in hope. They are not bound by form or rhythm, but by feeling. In these pages, you will find the echoes of love in its many shapes—tender, unrequited, fading, and fierce. You'll walk with me through grief and the hollow silences it leaves behind. You'll sit beside my loneliness, where the world feels distant, but thoughts are loud. You'll hear the restless voice searching for purpose, and glimpse the flicker of dreams still burning in the dark. This is not just poetry. This is a conclusion of moments lived, emotions weathered, and thoughts carried— sometimes too heavily—for too long. It is my attempt to make sense of being human, to give language to the things we often struggle to name.
If you see parts of yourself here, I hope you feel less alone. If you don't, I hope you still listen. Either way, thank you for being here, and for allowing my voice to reach yours.

Hoping for a Joyful Tomorrow, for All

Love & Hope

Mona

Acknowledgements

This book is the result of not just my efforts, but the love, strength, and support of the people who stood beside me when I needed it most.
To Tara, thank you for being my unwavering source of hope and strength. In the face of every obstacle, your belief in me helped me hold on and keep going.
To Rohit, your constant faith in me meant more than words can say. Thank you for recognizing my need to do more, to understand deeper, and for guiding me with patience and insight as I learned and grew.
To Betty, you were there when I faltered, pushing me forward whenever I got stuck. You never let me give up, especially during the lowest points of my life. I'm endlessly grateful for your presence, your persistence, and your heart.

Each of you helped shape this journey—and for that, I am truly thankful.

1. My Fairy Tale

Once upon a time, two winters away, i sat thinking by
the fire..
How would it have been if, if life had no desire
And then i thought of the forgotten years, The vision of
my dreams was so clear
The lullaby that put me off to sleep, a distant memory, a
locked treasure...
The man, who was my all and more, the one who shaped
my future?
Did u breath your last, thinking of me in this stupor?
All i can wish and hope and pray is, all that i can manage
You left me without a trace of fear and your smile was
the saving grace

All you gave was the charm and laughter and the
desperation of love
It took me a life-time to unravel the mysteries of your
riddle

Now that i feel i know the truth, the darkness is all but
gone
And yet i can't forgive you the treason, but it still makes
me smile evermore..

The lessons that i learnt were too heavy on my heart,
and my tears too dry
The caress of a stranger, i mistook as love and gave my
all too soon
My quest for love was all too consuming and yet i never
gave up
Did you ever think of your little girl?
the transition from "you" to "me" so soon?
Or are you running away again, leaving me in
despair............

1. Is this a Dream?

Is this a Dream?
Is it mine? Or this is a dream?
A dream filled with a thousand rainbows..
A rainbow, the true colour of love
A pot of gold is the reward

Then gold-digger i am, his smile is my treasure
My breath comes short, and my heart fills with pleasure
The smile that had me undone alll along
And yet it feels the same...
The silver thread that holds us together
Is just a rhythm of despair
The hair he so loved and cherished and kissed
The colour and the shine he desired
But alas! He took all the lustre
And left me without a fire

My life is all i had to offer

And yet it seems so little
The thunder in my heart gets louder
And yet I feel so brittle

Love goes and comes as it may
Shredding my thoughts apart
Rekindling the sparks that I knew were dead
To undo me again and dying with a broken-heart……

2. My Light

You are the sight of my eyes, the eyes that knew only the
dark..
You are the spirit behind my soul, the one that makes my
heart soar..

The light you bring in my life, brightens my heart and
makes me cry
Oh! Without you how will it be?
My days would be the same as night..............

U'd make me blind and yet
U're the one who has to try
Its all in your hands my love!
And you'll make me love and cry.

How cruel is your heart? To make me grieve
The death of my breaking-heart
A lonely tear is all i can spare

And yet i try not to fall apart

6

4. Escape

Escape

You are my escape, my soul my heartbeat,
You are the heart that keeps beating for me
You are the empty sighs and the secret smiles and
You are everything else i hoped for........

You are the hope that i dreamed for
You are the rhythm for my soul and my unfinished
melody,
you are the one who i've been meant for
You are my everything my all for ever more....................

You are my thoughts that keep me awake,
You are the blanket that keeps me warm in cold
December nights
You are the dream that i keep fighting for
And that is why; you are my reason to be

You are the hand that holds me

You are the smile that lifts my spirits
You are my hard day's labour
You are the ache deep down in my heart
You are my all, my destiny........................

4. The Smile of "me"

The smile of 'me'

Have you seen the smile of a child
Whose life is all but dark
The magic of life seems so near
And yet his touch can hurt

The tears of sorrow and of mourning,
Is so much a part of life
That the dear little boy embraces it all
And smiles his 'smile' as a warning

His eyes are shut and lips quivering
A prayer is all he can manage
His tear-drops are like crystal-ice
His face has me unnerving

The fervent kiss, and his loving touch
Is all that matters to me
The boy who was mine and yet unseen

Oh! Its all a dream for me

What i'd give to hold him tight
And never to lose his sight
And yet he is so far apart
And so i know he'll always be in me

I strain my eyes and cry my tears
Breaking my heart one more crack
The blind sweet boy is all i want
And now i've lost him, because i fear!!

5. The Storm

Is it just me, or is the world falling apart
Destruction is all i can see
A storm is rising in my heart
And yet the world is crying

The rain-drops remind me of 'me'
A faraway 'me' i knew
The splashes and the laughter is all there too
And yet the smile is missing!!

Is it me, or is the world falling apart
I hear the destiny's drum
Is it my heart, that is trembling
Or its just another dream

The silence before the storm makes me fear
For what tomorrow will bring
I can see myself, a smile on my lips

And yet my eyes are crying
The tears fall at random, with my heart's rhythm
The storm that i feared has come at last
With it, my sorrow will wash away
My herat will go on, in a tandom

I wont miss a beat or a sigh
My heart will love its flutter
Ah! The sweet kiss of death
Is all that can matter
Oh! Is it me, or is the world falling apart?

7. My meaning , My life

I know not, what you mean to me and the tie that holds
us together
The rosy sheen is back again and the feeling is there
forever
The thought of loosing you let my eyes wander, to the
never-ending light of day
My heart beat is the echo of my mind, my every breath
leads me to my blunder

The eyes can see him and shed its silent tears,
prospecting on its way as always
The heart is mine and so is the sorrow, My laughter can
never hide away my tears
Is it simple to feel the way i feel? Or is love always as
painful as this?
The sweet and tender poison engulfs me more like a
magic maze

8. Is it love?

Do i love you at all or is it a sense of shame, my heart is
all i have and yet i wonder
The thoughts that cross my mind are hard to tame, and
so i feel, your life'd be better if only i was kinder

Kind I can be, and full of tenderness too, the injustice of
fate is what i cant bear
Your love is all that i ever needed, yet your simple heart,
fills me with despair

Have i done the right thing and chosen the path, i so
thought was best
My mind's a clutter of the faraway past, and the burden
of the present is so much to bear
Whatever i do, or say or don't, my thoughts of you are
clear
At the deepest and the darkest hour of need, yours is the
only voice i can hear

Will you forgive me? For forgiveness is all i need, maybe
it can help...
Without your touch and the strength of your love, My
life will have no meaning whatsoever

9. Love

Love teaches us to be patient and kind
`Deep in the recess of my heart, lies a dormant dream
Distant although its light-years away
Where love comes only in whispers the hapless treasure ,
that I so desire....
Igniting the flames that were long forgotten, in to a
abyss of a pit-less mind
Wandering into the woods and waiting for the soft
caress of the night,
I lie awake, troubled and waiting, something.....anything
almost all for peace,
And yet it is "I", ...eyeing the starlit sky, counting
them in my fingers
Hoping a little............praying more than ever

Every time the story is repeated over and over again,
My tears fall freely soaking me completely

As though, all i could do is nothing but wrong, breaking
the dams of my soul
It comes in secret and washes me ashore but still my
arms are bare...............
I beg and plead, forgiveness is all i seek, love was never
meant to be.............
This perfect picture is what gets me in the end, lurking
in the dark
I get ready to fall, keep falling again, till the lies don't
stop.............
Then one fine day, all I've left is a tortured, poor little
heart...

I know this might come as a surprise "me" and the tear
streaked face.......
I spare you of my mind "dear-heart" as its a desolate
place
Alone is how i'm and what i like to be through the
tremors of the heart
A feeling, conquers all, isolates my sorrow drowning me
further below the ice

10. Such is Life!

Does it make me cry or fill me up with sorrow, I guess I'd
never know
Such is life....................My Love
The path we seldom cross, the stones we leave unturned
Is all that we remember tomorrow.

The cloud that gave us shelter and put us off to sleep;
Lullaby's aren't enough for the burden, for there are
promises yet to keep
The cross we bare and the paths we lead are often what
makes us stumble
Bumping and hurting we follow the light and end up in a
maze
The skeletons of the closet are finally put to rest,
No magic, tales or potions, I've put them all for a test.
The wine you offered as I broke my bread, the light we
shared and glowed
You were always there in my heart My Love,

It was "I", always I, that makes me wonder

19

11. My Knight in "Shining Armour"

You are my knight in shining armour, the light that
catches my heart
Your ready smile and the soft caress, is all for me, so I
surrender
The kind, love-filled eyes, is what draws me to you
It is this feeling, the satisfaction of "being", is what stops
me from a blunder

Without you love, where would I be, desolate and lonely
The party is in your honour, the music is yet to begin
Our lives have started just now, we have miles yet to go
The love I see deep in your eyes, tells me everything I
need to know
It touches my soul and brings me joy, the kind I've never
known before
My Knight, My Love, you make me complete, I Love You
ever more......

12. Loveless Heart

I love you "Love", is that what you want to hear?
my loveless heart has nothing to despair
the pieces all fall in place, the puzzle can solve itself
but the desolate, emptiness in my heart, you cannot
repair....
I love you, as love is all I have in me, I love you as loving
is all I can do.
I wonder at times if my life is true, my dreams real,

Or is it the beginning of a charming affair.
Affair it can be, if only they last for ever, for I have no
value for casual flings
My life has sought its mate for ever, And so I refuse to
give it all up without the fervour.........
Without the wishing & and praying & hoping for real
How could I love you, if Love is not for real...............?

13. Burning Tears

I have tears in my eyes and a heavy heart, and the clouds
seem to mirror my love
The cluster that feels my own and the thoughts that
crowd my mind
Are here to stay and torment what little is left of "me"
Alas! I wonder, is this what I dreamt of; when I was
younger?

I had dreams, wishes and aspirations too
That someday, it will all be mine...............
I would be my own fate and destiny
Alone is what I can be......................

Then you came stumbling into my life, like a breath of
fresh air
The Emptiness that was locked within, found its destiny
The love you shared and embraced me in a circle
Made me forsake my life and change me for ever

Did you realize the depth of your thoughts, when u
asked my hand for "U"
My soul was stirred and my thoughts started to
mingle.....
My laughter had a magic charm as it all fell in place
Although my life was waiting with bated breath.........
For this wonderful embrace..

14. Impossible Dreams..

When I sit, lost in my thoughts, wondering if my
dreams'll ever be true
A tiny voice inside of me, reminds me of all that is
new....
The feeling inside me grows with a fervent pitch
It tells me to be patient and yet I Wait for evermore....

I like to dream impossible dreams and wish for them
with all my heart
The lie, deceit and complications makes me forget my
part
I think life was simple and my heart was true
The dreams kept coming, and they made me get it
through.............

When the shadows linger, and hope seems a distant hue
I close my eyes tightly, daring to dream anew...
With every heartbeat whispers of courage softly call

This urge to rise and chase the light, to conquer every
fall

I like to weave my wildest hopes, release them to the
night
For in the dark where stars are born, my doubts can take
their flight
Though challenges may cloud the view, and fears begin
to fray
I'll hold onto the magic, believe in a brighter day..........

Undo my
life..............like it has never been before
Unwind my mind, let the troubles and worries go
Untie the ropes around my heart and make me die in
sorrow
Unblock the path that leads me to a better tomorrow....

If I ever think of the past, make me think of the good
times not the sad
If tears threaten to flow make the feelings borrow my
heart
If this is all that life has to offer, make me not wait for
what is not "mine"
For Love is right in front of me, let me grab it, there's so
little time
In every moment holds a chance, to love and to be freed.

15. Dying on my mind...

Lying on my bed, watching the stars twinkle at their will
My heart is heavy and so is my mind
I have moments I cherish, memories that refuse to fade
And yet the end is near, all I can do is watch & wait
In shadows' embrace, where silence echoes loud,
I trace the outlines of dreams beneath our shroud.
A fleeting touch, a whisper lost in time,
Reminds me of the rhythm, the pulse, the rhyme.

When I take my final breath, let the air be warm
I still have things and stuff to do
The pictures on my walls remind me of "you"
The times we knew were not so little and few
But seasons change and love can drift like leaves,
Yet in this heart, your laughter still weaves.
I search the night for signs we're not alone,
In the starlit silence, your spirit feels like home.

You should get over me, let the good times stay
I'll be forever yours and yours I'll always be
The regret that'll deeply be etched in my heart
Is : I wish we'd saved our love and listened to our heart
So as I linger in this tender night's sigh,
Know that though we part, our memories will fly.
With heavy heart, I'll always carry your grace,
In every heartbeat, in every empty space.

We were true and kind and patient with all that needs be
done
We made our lives the perfect heaven but you still had
me undone
Every time I look into your eyes, I see the pain I caused
The final touch and your kiss, was your "Good bye" but
you paused....

Did you feel my heart as it breathed its last ?
Did you hold my hand and cry ?
Did it hurt, to let me go and my memories ?
Or did you wish to, give it another try ?

16. Dearheart...

If you take all my sorrows, if you take all my pain
Do you think it'll be worth, sharing all the shame.......?
Without the thoughts to torment me and fill me up with
sorrow
How'd you think I'd live my life, with not a single thing
to borrow

The tears give me strength and make me lead the way
The emptiness is all I have 'cause it's the only
way...............
Life's been tough & difficult without your love and
constant care
I knew not what to do, if you were not there

The pain I try to hide so hard, creeps in by the night
....
It gives me nightmares and sleeplessness, i try and fight
it with all my might

The memories play its vicious part, and the rainbow
coloured hair
the first rain, the smell of autumn, doesn't seem all that
fair

When I look out of my window, the world looks nice and
friendly
A moment of understanding and defeat, can show the
colour of Ugly
The dew drops early in the morning, looks like crystal
beads
My life without you Dearheart, is almost as if my heart
bleeds

Yet I gather pieces of
courage, though shattered they may be,
In shadows of the memories, your love, it still haunts me.
As I weave through days of longing, I cling to whispered
dreams,
In the echoes of the silence, your laughter softly gleams.

17. Crazy heart

Me and my crazy little heart often think alike.......
We live in a world of make-believe and cherish what we
like
Every time there is a new beginning and an end....
Every thought that crosses my heart takes me to the
bend......

We wage our secret battles and wear our scars as badges
The turmoil inside the poor little heart, know not what it
causes...
The laughter and the snide remarks all hits its mark
Sometimes I believe that its fighting in the dark.........

It hurts me to know that you don't understand....
My life, my love and my sacrifice.........
The pain that sears my heart and makes it cry
The crushing point where its, needless to try...........

There will come a day when all of this would cease to
feel
And my heart will turn to ice
But till such day, I would hope and pray
And let my fate roll the dice.....

18. I don't love you...

I Don't Love You, Darling

(Or Maybe I Always Have)

I don't love you, darling...
Or maybe I just don't know how.
The feelings were soft, like whispered light,
Yet the words refused to come out loud.
One glance from you—those eyes, that smile—
And suddenly I forget to breathe.
You spin my world, undo my calm,
And plant wildflowers underneath.
I don't love you, darling...
Because love feels too small a name.
You, who drift like poetry through time,
Unaware you've sparked a flame.
Each thought of you unwraps my soul,
Like letters never meant to send.
And though I've failed to hold you right,
Your love—too kind—would still not bend.
I once believed that time could heal,

That fate would thread us close once more.
But life, in all its quiet ways,
Left pieces of us by the door.
Still in the hush between two beats,
I feel you like a silent prayer.
In every shadow, every light—
You're there, you've always been there.
I've searched the stars, the sky, the sea,
But nothing answered quite like you.
My heart forgot its rhythm, love—
Until your touch pulled it back through.
This tale began with open hands,
But the end was never set in stone.
I don't love you, darling...
I only ache where you've once shone.
But if you asked, I'd start again—
With trembling hope, with love renewed.
For what we share defies the rules—
It's quiet, deep, and achingly true.
So take my hand, and let us try,
No promises, just hearts laid bare.
We have a song, a fire, a dream—
And I still believe in love that dares.

19. I know not what I did

I hear you, I feel you true; the heart knows you'll be
there
For what seems like a lifetime, is seldom fair...
The smile that I hide in my eyes
Butteflies that flutter, awakens the only desire
In the stillness between heartbeats, your eyes find mine,
In whispered words, our souls entwine,
With every gentle sigh, you mend my broken threads,
A tapestry of dreams where love's light spreads.

And when the world is heavy, with shadows cast around,
Your laughter dances softly, a sweet, familiar sound,
I close my eyes, let the warmth pull me near,
In this sacred space, everything is clear.

Before you, love! I knew not what life had to offer
The thoughts that'd crossed my heart had no fire
Life's been crazy and surely a burning hell
I'm glad for once that I had you, to ring the bell

The bell that sent shivers down my spine
And had me reeling with unshed tears
Honey! You've given me everything & more
I've finally learnt to be without my fears.......

You are my all and the reason for my new found glory
You are the outlet for my pent-up fury
I beg of you darling! Do not judge me silly
I'd give my life, if only you'd understand me, really

I know there are times, I might be hard to read
The times you feel the cause is lost.......
And yet those are the times, I'm almost close
Waiting for U with bated breath
I look for you at times of need and wait for the look that
calms my nerves
You touch my hand and smile at me, Feels like there's
still a chance tomorrow...

Together we'll weave stories, from sunlit dawns to
night's embrace,
In the depths of our silence, I've found my place,
For in your gaze, I see the stars align,
Every heartbeat echoes, "You are forever mine.

20. Sometimes

Sometimes, the tear-drops fall like shooting stars,
Sometimes, I wonder if I'm still alive
Sometimes, words come out without a meaning
And sometimes, my face reflects its sorrow
Sometimes, shadows speak in whispers so loud,
Sometimes, I dream beneath an empty shroud.
Sometimes, laughter echoes in the silence deep,
And sometimes, I question the truths that I keep

Sometimes my heart beats an unknown rhythm
Sometimes I smile through all my tears
Sometimes life makes me wonder yet again
Is this the breeze that dragged me to my plunder
Sometimes, the dawn breaks with a heavy sigh,
Sometimes, I reach for stars that flicker and die.
Sometimes, the night wraps me in a tender embrace,
And sometimes, I roam in search of my place.

Sometimes emotions run raving wild, a tempest's wrath,
Sometimes, I walk along this fractured path.
And sometimes, the heart finds strength in the small,
Yet sometimes, it's in the silence I feel most small.

How life twists and turns and makes you face your facts
Sometimes emotions run raving wild.............
Sometimes the heart forgets to flutter,
and the butterflies start to slumber...........
Sometimes it is "I", only me that stops the heavens from
falling,
But sometimes, I wish to hear the stars calling.

21. If only

If only I could live in my dreams
Many fantasies I would have had by now,
Many castles, dwarfs and magic spells
Would have been my power by now
If only dreams are not brittle thoughts
If only they need no nurturing & care
What would have been a dream if all was still
And only If I could've had it all.....................

A knight with a heart that rivals the stars?
Riding through shadows, embracing the night,
Or perhaps a wanderer, simple yet true,
Whispering secrets the moonlight imbues.
if wishes were horses, where would they roam?
On fields of pure dreams, would I find my home?
In lands forged of stardust, where wishes take flight,
As magic and wonder weave threads of delight.
Yet here in this moment, I linger and sigh,

For dreams are the whispers of what could imply...
That even in waking, my heart still can soar,
If only I dared to dream even more.

22. Today

Today i feel like nothing of yesterday, today i feel no
pain
Today my sorrow is all but gone, or washed away in the
rain
The water that flows from my eyes the light that shines
through them
Its mystic its magical, how a simple life could be turned
around
Today my spirit rises like a bird unchained, flying high
in the blue
Today I dance with shadows of the past, no longer afraid
of what I knew
The sun wraps around me, shining bright, igniting
dreams from within
With each step forward, I embrace the journey, letting
the magic begin

All this time i thought in my mind and made my plans to
flee
All this time it was a distant dream but now is the time
to be free
All this time, I waited for the dawn, where every
heartbeat starts anew
All this time, the whispers called me forth, to chase the
vibrant hues
With open arms, I greet the light, my hopes are now my
guide
The path I see and hope to tread is where my wildest
dreams reside

All this time, I longed for the spark that would set my
spirit free
Give me a chance, oh! Once in my life, to taste the sweet
serenity
I've weathered storms, I've faced the night, let me bask in
morning's glow
If this is my time finally, then let the winds of fortune
blow[
I've toiled enough and bore the brunt of the world
If this is my time finally, then please let me see
Let me feel that I too can smile and live a life without the
misery

Does it really matter if this is real?
Does it matter, if only a fleeting scent?
If just for a moment, I can grasp the dreams that glimmer
like the stars,
Don't you think, it'll fill the void that life once lent?

23. How do I look?

Do I look, as if i'm about to smile
Smile as if to light the world beneath
Do I look old, for I have many memories
And sorrows hidden in my eyes...................
Do I look, like the blind boy with a smile on his lips?
Or

Do i ever look, happy and make you feel like smile?
Or Do I look, lost in my thoughts and tears brimming
over?
Do I wear the mask of hope, though threads are frayed?
Can you sense the shadows dancing just beneath my
skin?
Do I look like the sun might rise again, if only for a
while?
Or does my silence echo louder than the whispers of
despair?
Do I look as if my soul is searching for a place to land?

Or am I merely here, a ghost of who I used to be?
In every fleeting glance, do you see the pieces lost?
Or am I just a fleeting thought, a moment in your day?
Tell me again, my love, do I look as if I'm afraid to cry?

Or
Do I seem resilient, holding shadows at bay

Do i look, as if life has just begun and ended right before
my eyes
Or can you see the pain too??
Do I look, like someone who's lost a loved one,
Or someone who still grieves.............
My tears are dry and lips are sealed
And yet my heart is falling apart
Tell me my love ?
Do I look as if, I'm about to FLy........

24. Life........

Have you ever wondered, what life is all about?
A thousand dreams, a thousand memories are stored
within
Undoing the past and foreseeing the future
And being what you are somehow
Its hard to trust or understand the logic behind this
Yet we seem to believe it all without much credence
But hope flickers softly beneath the weight of despair,
A faint whisper that beckons me to look beyond the
shadows.
If only I could grasp the threads of tomorrow,
Weaving a tapestry of dreams unfurled, of endless
possibilities

Each heartbeat resounds like a promise unmade,
Songs of joy lingering in the silence of the night.
So tell me, moon, will you light the path ahead?
Will your glow guide the weary souls back home?

The breath we take and the air we feel are all a part of us,
Its a miracle, this beautiful world and we still forsake
this
In the stillness, I whisper secrets to the stars,
Hoping they'll carry my wishes to the winds of change.
For in this maze of life, I seek a ray of solace,
To cradle my heart amidst the chaos that surrounds.

The smile and tenderness is so very rare these days
Its like the sky has opened up with all the stars beneath
it
The tears are blinding me as I wait
For all the faith to come back to me again
Thats all i have a few empty night,
I spend them all in misery filling all my doubts

25. Sand – Castles

If there was a place called "home"
Thats where I'll always be
Out in the open with a cup of coffee steaming
With a book on my lap and my eyes on the ocean's
dreaming
That's where I'll always be.............

If home is what i dream of often
Then my life is such a sorrow riddle
For I've looked far and wide and everywhere
And yet it remains a mystery, a game I can't fiddle

There is a house I know of, not far from here
All it takes, is a few short steps
And i feel the waves splashing, their laughter sincere
The tide has risen and so have my hopes
it crumbles beneath my feet
And Time slips away, like whispers, like breaths

I make my castles big and small,
Filled with turrets and dungeons, realms of my own
And yet I want to dream like an angel
In a twilight world where love has grown..

They say don't make castles in the air
Or dream of a knight in a shining armour bright
They know not what it is:
To wait for someone, and know that they are always
near, A guiding Light.

26. Walking Alone

When darkness filled my life and my sight was all but
gone....
A flicker, a ray, a hope is all I waited for
Down in the dungeons of my long lost soul
Searching for the lamp, the one that'll brighten my day..
Along the shores, the bridge of shells open....
Was it the light in your eyes that guided my way?
Or has time woven itself into a tapestry of dreams?[
The breeze gives me inspiration and the palm trees
beckon

In shadows I linger, a whisper of what lies ahead,
I walk along its shiny path, wonder in my eyes and my
breath caught in my heart
So I gather the moments, both fragile and bright,
Embroidering hope with the threads of my fears.
With each step I take, I unearth the soft light,
A flicker that dances, dissolving my tears.

For your love is the lantern that threads through the
night,
A promise that sways on the edge of the dawn.
Though the road may be winding, and shadows may bite,
In your arms, I find solace, a place I belong.

I

The journey we shared is far from over and so my heart
says...
May I steal my thoughts and wait for ever?
Bittersweet memories are all the treasure I carry
Your heart and a hint of a smile.............
The anger I so cherished and the hurt locked away..
You made me whatever I've become today
And that just makes me wonder...................

27. Desire

The look, the soft touch, our hands felt it all...................
When i saw the truth in your eyes,
My mind kept reeling back and forth, memories passing
by....
Our love needs no words or a hint of a consolation
We are together and thats all that I care
In this fleeting moment, nothing else matters,
Just the warmth of your presence, just the spark in the
air

The silence of our spirits......................
Our souls unite, maybe someday, I can hope and pray
Its only these small little treasures that I save
Deep within my heart, is it locked away?
In whispers of dreams, your laughter calls me near,
A melody unspoken, yet I can hear it clear.

Questions, I have loads and yet the fright it gives
Am I, what i think I am?
The ripple I saw, maybe was all my fault,

Loving you was not my choice and yet it felt right
Is there a reason, a meaning for this constant fear
My heart keeps longing for you, and yet I despair...
But in the shadows, hope flickers bright,
A flame that endures, even in the night.

My love, you know it all and yet you hold your ground
You turn me to ice and wait for what is yours
Eons I kept lying about, feels like a bag of dreams
Yet you get back to me with all tenderness, as if it was
never been
I trust your spirit, our souls unite once more
This time I pray, how I wish, may you never leave.
Hold me close, in this dance of fate so divine,
For together, my love, we'll write our own sign.

28. Leaving You

I'm leaving you today, so your tomorrow is new.....
The weight I carry with me is too much to bear.......
My love will always be with you and so is my spirit........
But my heart, I've to go, and that's all I can share

My memories cloud my mind and make your days only
trouble
I'm here in your arms with dreams filling my eyes.....
The darkness shrouds me in its cloak
And I'm left with an overbearing choice...........
Yet whispers of hope linger, a faint, flickering light.........

If I leave you and let you be, you'll know sorrow never
Your heart shall sing or dance in rhythm
My touch you will forget and learn to smile
And bid me "Goodbye" for ever....
As the dawn breaks anew, casting shadows to flight...

I know now what tears my eyes are hiding......
I've but one unfinished mystery left behind

Life can go on and on even if I don't
Through it all I've seen the truth and that's
What my heart should follow.................

The path is lonely, dark and long..........
Yet this is where I belong...........
The laughter leaves my eyes as i surrender
This is what I should've done at the start
But I let my heart take its course and wander........
Now with a bittersweet farewell, my soul can finally
depart.......

29. Oh! Love

Is it true ?............that love makes you wise
Then why do I still love you I wonder.....
Lessons I learnt, stories I heard, made me promise
Not to give my heart to a stranger..............
Yet here I am, lost in your gaze's embrace,
Drowning in tides of your unspoken grace.

Your charming ways blinds my heart
And fills it with desire
I know I'll walk with you now.........................
And my life would be my burning pyre
For every flicker, whispers of love's cruel game,
Ignite the shadows, stoke the flame.

How could i be blind and lead you on?............
How could we share so many dreams?
How should I forget the promises you made?.............
The ones you had thought you would keep
And in the silence, echoes of your name haunt me still,
Chasing phantoms through the night, against my will.

How many nights have u lain awake?.........counting stars
Wondering what had become of me?
Should i trust you and let you make me smile?
Should I give you the power to be?...............
Or will you fly away as the winters approach?
Forget me again, my sweet little liar?...............
Or will you anchor my heart where hope won't expire?

30. New Beginnings

I let my tears fall at random,
I let you walk away every night............
Loving you is all I can do,
And love is: my only desire.....

The footsteps you leave in my heart
Impressions do they make
Every time I hear the breeze
I feel you around me and memories do they make
Every time my heart is in a tangled mess
I look around for you
For you are the only one who can make me cry
Maybe it is the end, but I'll give another try...

I'm patient and kind at times when I look at you
Your face is the mirror of your soul, yet you never
knew....
I see Love, Pain and Desperation
Its all there for all to witness and still u don't care

My heart is strong and it will beat forever for you
But I'm aware, the last few steps are for you to take
Loneliness I know only too well........
You cant drown me in your sorrows, I've gone through
so........

if there's something you wish to say and feel your
thoughts stammer...
Know it deep within your heart, that's how my heart'll
also hammer...
So spare me the hurt and silent tears, for I don't care
anymore
My heart is full of happy memories,
And that I cant, no more despair..........
Yet in the quiet, I still hear your name,
Whispers of what was, they flicker like a flame.
In the tapestry of dreams, your thread still entwines,
But I'm learning to weave new patterns, beyond tangled
lines.

31. Listless Mind

Let me live with broad open eyes, unchained from the
dark
Let joy weave through my days like sunlight through
leaves,..
Let love not cloud my mind and embrace my heart
Let me live with broad open eyes............
Let my dreams spread its wings across the
oceans...Soaring high
Let love not give it all up, but nurture the spark
Let my spirit dance freely, in rhythm, in its rhythm..

I want to fly away and feel the sky, unconfined
And jump into the deepest ocean, where the secrets
dwell
I want to smile like a child with a million dreams, pure
and bright
And hope to someday feel alive, in every heartbeat's
swell.

My want for a tiny picket fence, a haven to hold dear
My wish to tread alone, where whispers sway
To feel the early morning drops, they sparkle like fresh
tears
How life is what we mean and dream in every fleeting
day
But for me its my only miracle, my heart's refrain

32. The reflection: thats me..

I saw her walking down the stairs...........
I saw her frail hands and her flares....................
The tears in her eyes were brimming over
Her enchanting smile beckons me.................
Filling me with hope, love and maybe despair....

Will she know me, feel my presence now that i'm here
Or will I be just another blank stare,
She looks at me and yet away
Maybe hiding away the pain
The memories that cloud her mind
Makes her fear, but all for nothing, no gain.............

She sees me with unseeing eyes
As if her life is all but gone...................
Tired and broken and a hollow heart......................
Shines for me like a beacon...

I look at her and feel her pain
And cross my hands to pray................
"God ! " I fear let this not be "me".........
For I don't have the strength to bear...

I open my eyes and witness the morning sun....
And cherish the warmth I feel
And soon I know my day would come............
The very same stairs one day, would be waiting just for
me.......

Yet in this moment, I hold my breath tight,
For shadows whisper secrets of the night.
A heartbeat away from the light that fades,
I long to guide her through memory's maze.

What if we meet where the lost souls find rest?
Where hope entwines with dreams, surely blessed?
Together we'll rise, as our spirits transcend,
In the embrace of dawn, where love knows no end.

33. I'm every Girl

I'm every girl, behind every shadow...............
Behind the veil......
I'm every girl, with brilliant dreams...............
A girl who lives by what she believes.....
A girl who doesn't know tomorrow........

I'm every girl, with wide eyed passion
Not a thought has marred my vision..........
My cloud and the silver lining......................
And my tears are my celebration

I'm every girl, you meet and smile
I'm every girl in every manner...................
I'm the girl who cares not of the future or the
mysteries....
Who waits for the early morning sun......
Whose eyes are moist with tears.........
Yet finds strength in the dawn's gentle light......

I'm the girl who laughs out loud at petty things......
And cries when the sky's brimming..............
For I'm the only girl who makes you smile.............
Although her heart inside is dying.........
Masked by joy, yet the burden is heavy...............

I'm every girl, who walks and holds your hand
The girl who just knows you more..............
For she lives inside your beating heart.............
For she's the one who'll hear your pain and endure....
Bearing your sorrows as if they were hers......
Creating hope where shadows conspire to obscure...........

34. This is you...

You cant make up your mind and choose the path meant
for you
You keep looking back and re-living memories of the
past........
Memories that gave you love and happy times.....
Memories that'll also break your dear little heart.....
Caught in a whirlwind of choices, we dance in circles
anew,
With threads of joy interwoven, yet shadows tug at
you......
Each laughter rings like echoes through the corridors of
time.....
But whispers of regret entwine, a haunting, silent
crime....

You cant fail and yet you know the battle cant be won.....
You keep trying in desperation and fill your heart with
hope....

For you believe your day will come and you may get the
clue....
But try as you might, you cant forgive the past, for you
cant win them true...
You stand at the crossroads, where dreams clash and
collide.....
With whispers of your heart's desire, yet fear you cannot
hide....
For every step is laden with the footsteps you've
outgrown.....
And all the love you nurtured, now feels like a heavy
stone.

You spoke to me and held my hand when you finally had
to go
You dared me with your eyes and your hugs told me
so........
Your heart could feel it, "yes" I know it all...............
Yet you chose to ignore the truth and bore the brunt of
your fall
You gave me solace in your gaze, a promise soft and
bright,
Yet masks we wore around our hearts turned day into
endless night.....
I felt the truth unspoken still lingered in our space,
A solitary tear cascaded, in longing's tight embrace......

If you want to wait for me till I'm frail and old......
My love I can guarantee, I'll lose my hope, if truth be
told.....
I've waited all my life and maybe lifetimes too....
Let my heart, not pay the price for trying ever more...
If you want to wait for me till the stars start to fade......
I fear the twilight shadows leave love's tender thread
frayed......
But if fate weaves our paths again in a realm where
dreams are pure,
I'll treasure every heartbeat, in the silence, we endure......

35. This is fate

This is fate and what I call destiny
This is my life and just my misery..............
Every time I want to look up and see the sky
You come into my life, sweep me up and fly.............

For the moment I know love and laughter is here....
For the moment I know, the truth is hiding near..........
You keep telling me, that all will be well...........
And my heart feels it Love, and makes it swell..........

I keep ignoring my eyes and block my ears of pain....
For this pain is real, this moment is all that you can spare
The hours and minutes with every second that goes by
My heart feels the sorrow and knows you are just
passing by.......

My love for you is only maybe a game ....
One that you love to play when you are here..........

So I know, I was not meant to be a part of you..........
But now this pain I can smile and bear........

I wish you had thought of sharing your sorrows with me
My life is yours and that's how it'll always be
No matter what, no matter when, I can pay the
price............
Loving you has given me all and this is my only Prize......
Yet there are shadows that dance in my mind's embrace,
Lingering whispers of love lost in time and space...........
Though your absence cuts deep, I gather my heart,
In this bittersweet symphony, we've played our
part.............

So I'll stand on this edge, with the wind at my back,
Embracing the silence, reclaiming what I lack..........
For every tear shed, there's a lesson I've learned,
In the ashes of longing, my soul will be burned..

36. I Love You so.............

If I love you so, that is not your fault.......
My heart don't seek yours in return...........
The want, the desire to love you, "My Love"....................
Is the only want that matters, if at all.....

Every time I look at you, love brimming in my eyes.....
You choose to look away, and yet my heart defies.....
I love you for being you, and that's not an ultimatum..
'Yes' or 'No' is not what I want ;
You ought to know, I love you with every single atom....

You are my life, my dreams my aspirations.....
You are the reason for I am "me'
You change the path my life could've chosen ......
Yet I couldn't fault you for the treason........

My love for you has no motive or condition.........
You are you and that is enough for me, a motivation....

Every word you say and the thought when it crosses
your mind...
My heart knows the need, the want and desperation...
I want to help but only you can try....
The test of life is long and hard so you mustn't cry...
If love is not what you desire and claim from me....
Then let me be with you, I can fulfil your dreams just
dare...
Love gives me strength, tears make me try....
Whatever your heart desires............
I promise you, will be yours, just let me try............

37. My Love for You

For love knows no bounds, it just seeks to fly.......
In whispered hopes, where our wishes align,......
Let my presence be the shelter from your stormy sea,.....
A quiet refuge, where you can just be me......

Though shadows may linger, I'll be your light,......
With every heartbeat, I'll stand by your side,......
If today feels heavy, I'll carry the weight,......
Together we'll navigate, we'll twice celebrate.....

Should your path be weary, and you feel lost in time,......
I'll weave your sorrows into verses sublime,......
For loving you freely, with no strings attached,......
Is a tapestry of truth, beautifully matched.....

So let our souls dance in the spaces between,......
Where love flourishes quietly, unseen but keen,......
With every glimmer of hope that we find,......
Know that I cherish you, in body and mind.....